IMPROVING WRITING SKILLS

S U R V I V A L   S K I L L S   F O R   S C H O L A R S

Managing Editor: Mitchell Allen

Survival Skills for Scholars provides you, the professor or advanced graduate student working in a college or university setting, with practical suggestions for making the most of your academic career. These brief, readable guides will help you with skills that you are required to master as a college professor but may have never been taught in graduate school. Using hands-on, jargon-free advice and examples, forms, lists, and suggestions for additional resources, experts on different aspects of academic life give invaluable tips on managing the day-to-day tasks of academia—effectively and efficiently.

Volumes in This Series

SURVIVAL SKILLS FOR SCHOLARS

IMPROVING WRITING SKILLS

Memos, Letters, Reports, and Proposals

ARTHUR ASA BERGER

SAGE Publications
International Educational and Professional Publisher
Newbury Park   London   New Delhi

Copyright © 1993 by Sage Publications, Inc.

For information address:

 SAGE Publications, Inc.
2455 Teller Road
Newbury Park, California 91320

SAGE Publications Ltd.
6 Bonhill Street
London EC2A 4PU
United Kingdom

SAGE Publications India Pvt. Ltd.
M-32 Market
Greater Kailash I
New Delhi 110 048 India

#28377490

Printed in the United States of America

Library of Congress Cataloging-in-Publication Data

Main entry under title:

Berger, Arthur Asa, 1933-
  Improving writing skills : memos, letters, reports, and proposals
/ Arthur Asa Berger.
      p.   cm.   — (Survival skills for scholars ; vol. 9)
  Includes bibliographical references.
  ISBN 0-8039-4822-0 — ISBN 0-8039-4823-9 (pbk.)
  1. Business writing. 2. Commercial correspondence. I. Title.
II. Series.
HF5718.3.B47   1993
808'.06665—dc20   93-11405
                                                            CIP

93 94 95 96 10 9 8 7 6 5 4 3 2 1

Sage Production Editor: Megan M. McCue

Contents

To my Minnesota mentors,
David Noble, Mulford Q. Sibley,
and Ralph Ross

Preface

Unlike Jay Gatsby, who sprang from a platonic conception of himself, most of us who work in universities and other academic institutions write ourselves into existence. (Or, at the very least, we write ourselves into folders in filing cabinets in various offices.)

We are asked to write many different kinds of documents: letters of recommendation for students, memos to colleagues, proposals and reports to administrators—the list goes on and on. And like Sisyphus, it often happens that as soon as we finish one document we are asked to write another one.

Each document generally has a specific format and contains certain kinds of information. This little guide discusses some of the more important kinds of memos, letters, reports, and proposals; offers many suggestions about writing them effectively; and describes the formats for each kind of document in some detail. It also deals with such matters as readability, collaborative writing, the process of writing and rewriting documents, and layout and design.

Effective Business Correspondence and Academic Success

For most of us who teach in colleges, universities, and other academic institutions, the ability to write good memos, letters, reports, and proposals (as well as other kinds of documents such as minutes for meetings) is crucial. This kind of writing will probably play a larger role in our careers and have more to do with our success than the scholarly research that many of us were trained to conduct and write about. Many of us, perhaps even most of us, are not at high-powered research institutions where the so-called publish-or-perish (or publish-*and*-perish, in some cases) rule applies.

Academic institutions exist to educate students and support professors who conduct research, but these are only some of many university and college functions. They also need to provide numerous services for their students and faculties. Running an academic institution, like any organization that may have thousands of workers (in this case, faculty and staff members and tens of thousands of students), requires a great deal of work, for there are decisions to be made about all kinds of matters.

Under the Iceberg:
Memos, Letters, Reports, and Proposals

Because universities are self-governing (at least in principle, if not always in practice) they form committees to take care of the things that need to be done: from making budgets to looking after emergencies, from reforming the general education curriculum to making departmental curriculum changes. There is often a good deal of disagreement (at every level and among different parties) about the curriculum, personnel decisions, and other matters. This means that faculty members (from instructors to professors) and administrators (from department chairs and associate deans to presidents) spend a good deal of time and energy writing memos and letters, preparing reports and proposals, and sending these documents to one another.

Curiously, graduate students are not generally taught very much about how to write effectively as members of educational institutions, just as they often do not take any courses on teaching. The theory is, I would imagine, that if you are intelligent enough to get an advanced degree, then you should be smart enough to figure out how to teach and how to write good memos and letters on your own.

Teaching Is What You Do When You Are Not Writing Memos

It often seems as if teaching and research get lost in the shuffle as professors and administrators crank out memo after memo. Teaching becomes what you do when you are not writing memos. (And becoming an administrator often means abandoning research and spending years writing memos, letters, reports, and proposals and attending meetings to discuss these documents.)

So it will be useful to learn something about writing good memos, letters, reports, and proposals—to make life easier for yourself and to help you with your career.

Remember, the written word lives—and you will live and, I hope, prosper if you are careful about the words you write. To a great extent, your fate is in your own hands.

A Few Words About Your Guide

This is the second book I have written on writing. I have taught writing for radio and television for many years and recently decided to write my own book on the subject because I did not like any of the other books that were available. So I wrote a book called *Scripts: Writing for Radio and Television* that is used in many institutions. It deals with the basic formats used in writing radio and television scripts and also has material on style and comedy writing. I also have written many articles and books on media, popular culture, semiotics, and humor.

A Final Note

I assume that you are a good writer. But every writer can benefit from a bit of advice from time to time, which is one reason why there are editors and copy editors. It also is convenient to have a book that provides detailed information about the contents of the various documents that you will be writing and that offers hints about everything from collaborative writing to sending E-mail. I hope that you will find this little book useful and that it will help you write better memos, letters, reports, and proposals.

ARTHUR ASA BERGER

PART I

Memos, Letters, Reports, and Proposals

1 | How to Write Better Memos

The memo is the basic communication form used in academic institutions. Letters, reports, and proposals can be seen as modifications and amplifications of the memo. *A memo, as it is traditionally defined, is a short written communication that is distributed internally in some organization and which is often written on a prepared form.* Letters, for our purposes, are written communications that are not generally distributed internally. Usually, memos are devoted to one subject, which explains why they tend to be short—often one page—but sometimes are considerably longer, such as when used as tenure and promotion "letters" (which actually are written as memos).

Writing Good Memos Is an Art

Writing is an art in which our personality, our sense of style, our knowledge, and our imagination play important roles. Everything we write reflects what we are like and reveals a great deal about us. Thus it makes good sense to do as good a job as we can with every memo we write. We may dismiss memos as being simple, relatively formulaic documents that are not worth much attention, but that is a big mistake. Each memo, whatever else it might be, is an advertisement for the memo writer.

When we write, we do several different things at the same time. While we engage in the actual process of writing words down, one after another, we also think about how these words and our ideas should be organized, consider strategies to achieve the effects we want, and tie all of this to various cognitive processes involving our knowledge base. All of these processes not only involve our rational decisions—this word and not that one—but also are affected by unconscious matters. That is why the documents we write do not always turn out the way we think they will. In the process of writing, we discover things we did not know we knew, which is why I find writing exciting and challenging.

We want to consider how to write with style, with grace, with felicity, with economy, and with purpose. Writing may have its mysterious aspects, because it is a creative art and we still do not understand the phenomenon of creativity. But there are many things we can do when we write to create better memos that are not mysterious (and also many practices we can avoid). What follows, then, is a guide to writing effective memos in academic institutions.

Typical Subjects of Memos

The following are among the more common kinds of memos we write in the course of our activities in academic institutions.

❶ *Reporting on decisions.* This memo might come from the administration and describe a course of action that is to be undertaken. Or it might come from a department's hiring committee and report that the department has voted to have an internal search for its chair or that its promotion committee has voted to support a given candidate for promotion.

❷ *Response to a memo from someone else.* Here the memo is written in reply to a memo from someone: offering information, explaining some action, and so on. Or the memo might amplify a previous memo.

❸ *Reporting on understandings reached in meetings or conversations.* A department might meet with a dean or somebody from another

---

Date: March 15, 1993
To: Dean A. Caligula
From: Jane Q. Public,
                  Assistant Professor, Conceptual Studies
Subject: Meeting of January 3, 1993

Thank you for taking time from a busy schedule to meet with me. I am very pleased that you will be supporting my effort to establish a conceptual studies laboratory and have promised support of $10,000 dollars for multimedia equipment to get it set up.

This laboratory will play a major role in enhancing the curriculum in conceptual studies and the reputation of our college in the university.

Figure 1.1. Memo

department about some issue and then send a memo reporting its understanding of what transpired—to set the record straight. Or a professor might have a meeting with the chair about some topic and send a memo recording his or her understanding of what transpired. Figure 1.1 is an example of such a memo.

The memo in Figure 1.1 does several things:

- It thanks the dean for his time (it is always a good idea to be nice to deans, especially if you are an assistant professor).
- It reminds him that he has promised money for your laboratory.
- In addition, it shows how the promised money will help the new laboratory contribute to the curriculum and the education of the students.
- It suggests the new laboratory will enhance the reputation of the college in the university (and, indirectly, the dean).

❹ *Minutes of meetings.* We often are called on to write minutes of departmental or committee meetings. Writing minutes is not a mechanical matter but one that calls for a great deal of discretion. You cannot write down every word, so you must consider what to include and what to leave out. In addition, you have to decide how to characterize discussions—keeping in mind that you have to be accurate, that you do not want to offend anyone in the meeting, and, finally, that others who have hostile intentions may see the minutes. Consider Figure 1.2, which shows different ways of characterizing what occurred in a meeting.

A boisterous, angry argument ensued with everyone screaming at one another . . .

versus

A lively discussion ensued with various positions being voiced . . .

and

The committee, after endless discussion, was hopelessly deadlocked on the issue . . .

versus

After a comprehensive analysis of the issue, the committee decided that more discussion was needed . . .

Figure 1.2.

When you write a memo covering a committee meeting you typically do the following:

- list the names of the people attending the meeting and, when relevant, their departmental affiliations;
- enumerate the topics discussed, say something about what was said, and briefly note what decisions were made; and
- write down any motions that were made, who made and seconded them, important points of the discussion that followed, and what the results of the voting on the motion were.

❺ *Memos that request something.* We often have simple requests to make. We want someone to do something for us, or we request relatively trivial sums of money. In these cases we write request memos. Figure 1.3 offers a request memo.

The memo in Figure 1.3 has the following attributes of good memos:

- It is short—fewer than 100 words.
- It is direct and starts by making a request.
- It is detailed—that is, it makes a specific request, offers an explanation of why the request should be granted, and suggests the consequences of granting the request.

The memo is the workhorse of academic writing and is used because it provides a record of decisions made and

Date:	April 15, 1995
To:	Miles Gloriosus,
	Associate Dean, School of Basic Studies
From:	David Hume,
	Instructor, Department of Theoretical Concerns
Subject:	Minigrant of $250

I would like a grant of $250 from your discretionary funds to complete a book tentatively titled *An Enquiry Concerning Human Understanding*. I have good reason to believe, though I cannot be certain, that this book will find a publisher and be of interest to a considerable number of people doing research in theoretical concerns and related matters.

Figure 1.3.

actions taken that can be used in the event of controversies, complications, or difficulties among parties involved in any transaction.

Rules for the Memo Writer

Now that we have considered the more important kinds of memos and things to keep in mind when we write them, let me offer some suggestions and cautions of a more specific nature that may be of assistance to you when you write any kind of document.

❶ *Consider every word in your memo.* Every word you use has its own connotations and resonates in different ways. In this respect, think about terms such as *every* and *each*:

Consider *every* word in your memo.
Consider *each* word in your memo.

If you look at these two sentences, you can see a subtle difference between them. The term *each* suggests careful attention to the language used in the memo, word by word, while the term *every*

What We Say	What We Mean
X shows great promise.	X hasn't done anything yet.
X plays by the rules.	X is rigid and inflexible.
X's work is very practical.	X's work has no theoretical value.
X is diligent, hard-working.	X isn't too smart.
X is an individualist.	X isn't a team player.
X is confident, self-assured.	X has a monumental ego.

Figure 1.4.

comprehensively lumps the words all together. If you want a bit more emphasis, you could write:

Consider *each* and *every* word in your memo.

❷ *Know your readers.* Aside from the simplest ones, most memos —especially those involving personnel matters or the allocation of funds to individuals or departments—are examined with great care by anyone who might be affected by the memo and decisions made relative to it. Thus you must be extremely judicious and take care that you do not inadvertently insult individuals or departments or that you expose yourself to attack by saying something that others (who may be competing with you or your department for scarce resources) can use against you.

❸ *Be polite.* Memos are written by people in academic institutions with different philosophies of education, different personalities, and different goals. Some have power to affect our careers. We have to take all these matters into consideration. Therefore the tone of memos should be polite, and generally they should be written in a formal manner. In some circumstances it may be acceptable to alter the tone of your memos, but for the most part it is better to be careful.

❹ *Be judicious.* It is often a good idea to use terms that say one thing but can be construed as meaning something else (see Figure 1.4). Sometimes we must write memos and letters that may be seen by the people we are writing about, memos that might possibly anger or upset them. In such situations, we have to write in a manner that is deliberately ambiguous. That is why memo writing is an art; one writes a memo that seems polite, civil, and positive and yet actually is critical and says or implies unpleasant things about someone's intelligence, character, or behavior.

❺ *Never send a memo or any document in haste.* It is human nature to want to send an angry response to actions by others or to memos that offend us. Indignation, righteous or not, can only get you in trouble. So write the memo, if you must, but then throw it away and write another memo that is less emotional and that you will not regret sending. And be sure to erase the angry memo from your computer files.

❻ *Consider carefully to whom the memo will be distributed.* Universities are bureaucratic institutions, which means that there are regular distribution channels for memos. You must devote a good deal of thought about to whom you will send your memos. A memo sent to both the dean and the president might get the dean angry, because you may not have followed the prescribed rules about the chain of command—who gets memos dealing with certain subjects and who does not. Send your memos where they will do the most good and refrain from sending them where there might be undesired damage. For example, if you publish an article, you might send a copy and an accompanying memo to your chair and the dean to remind them that you are a productive scholar.

❼ *Use colleagues in your department or some committee to edit and revise memos sent in their name.* Memos are often drafted by one person, who is writing it for a committee or a department. It is a good idea to have a committee colleague or someone in your department whom you trust go over the draft and make suggestions about your use of language, the reasons you offer for a particular position, and so on. You might also ask friends to review personal memos you write.

❽ *Avoid sexist and other offensive language.* Avoid gender-specific writing, which is characterized by the use of male pronouns (*he* and *his*) or female pronouns (*she* and *her*) (see Figure 1.5). The best way to avoid gender-specific pronouns is to use plurals such as *they* or *their*. Some writers use *s/he* and *his/her* in their work, but such usage gets to be extremely awkward. We also want to avoid sexist or gender-specific writing because it can suggest that women either do not exist or are irrelevant. In addition, we wish to avoid language that religious, racial, ethnic, sexual, or other groups find demeaning. (For example, when Ross Perot addressed a gathering of African-Americans, he naively used the phrase "you people," which many

Instead of	Use
chairman	chair, chairperson
coed	student
black	African-American
policeman	police officer
Indian	Native American
Eskimo	Inuit
deaf	hearing-impaired
handicapped	physically challenged

Figure 1.5.

in the audience found insulting. It was a major political blunder for him.) In recent years, thanks to the work of psychologists, linguists, and other scholars, we have become much more sensitive to the power of language and the way it affects people.

The Importance of Procedure

One of the most common ways that faculty members win battles with administrators is by showing that the administrators did not follow the procedural rules found in the faculty manual. The same applies to administrators who win battles with professors.

That is why everyone writes memos. They are placed in your file and in other files as well and can be used, if necessary, to demonstrate that official procedures were or were not followed. And that is why it is important to write memos that are detailed and complete and to keep hard copies of all the memos and other documents you send.

If men (and women) were angels, some have suggested, we would not need any government (although others have disputed that position). But men and women, whether they are assistant professors or university presidents, are not angels, so it is important to document everything you can in the event that you get involved in some kind of litigation—an

American disease—and must resort to grievance committees, arbitrators, or even, in some cases, lawyers and courts.

Printed Memo Forms

Academic institutions generally provide printed memo forms, under their letterheads, with the following:

Date:
To:
From:
Subject:

When it is being sent to more than one person, the end of such a memo often lists the people to whom the memo is being distributed after "cc:" (carbon copy). Memos are typically initialed or signed after or near where the name of the sender has been typed.

Conventions Followed in Writing Memos

Memos are usually written following these formatting conventions:

1. Paragraphs are not indented.
2. Each paragraph is single-spaced.
3. An extra space is placed between paragraphs.
4. Charts and informational graphics ("infographics") are used to organize data.
5. Right margins are not justified.

Most guides to writing advise not justifying the right margin; this avoids large gaps between words and islands of white space typically found in documents that are so justified.

Summary

In this chapter we have explored the intricacies of memo writing, the different kinds of memos, their formats, and their functions and considered their importance for us as "defensive" documents. In Chapter 2 we will examine the topic of letters. We are often asked to write letters of recommendation for our students or to write promotion letters for our colleagues. The next chapter not only focuses on these kinds of letters but also on such matters as the most common letter formats and writing with style.

2 | How to Write Effective Letters

Letters are written for the same purpose as memos: to give information, to state beliefs, to argue for positions . . . and, ultimately, to create a paper trail and provide documentary evidence that a professor, an academic administrator, an appeals board, a lawyer, or a judge (if things get to that stage) will find useful. In many cases, we use the terms *memos* and *letters* interchangeably; as mentioned in Chapter 1, so-called promotion letters are technically memos. We tend to use the term *letter* loosely to suggest matters of some importance.

For our purposes, letters are *written communications sent by university administrators, staff members, or faculty members to one another (internal letters) or to people outside academic institutions (external letters)*. Traditionally, memos are used for communications within an organization, but letters are also used when we want to suggest a greater degree of personal interest and significance or a greater sense of formality.

We now consider several kinds of letters of recommendation and promotion.

Letters of Recommendation for Students

We are commonly asked to write letters of recommendation for students who are applying for jobs or admission to graduate schools. In these letters we generally write about the following:

1. The courses the student took with us, whether the student was a research or teaching assistant, and how long we have known the student.
2. The performance of the student in our courses and, when applicable, as our assistants. We might also mention particular papers the student wrote and his or her contribution to class discussions.
3. The intellectual qualities and character of the student and a comparison of the student with other students we have taught and with whom we have worked.
4. Predictions for the student's future success in graduate school or in professional work as based on our experiences with the student.

We should avoid mentioning race, religion, ethnicity, age, and other matters of that nature.

Many institutions provide forms on which to write answers to specific questions; you may not even have to write a complete letter. In some cases it is useful to write a "To Whom It May Concern" letter for the student in which you deal with the topics listed above.

Now we will consider a much more complicated document: a promotion letter written to support a colleague who is a candidate for promotion. These letters are often 15 to 20 pages long. Figure 2.1 is a highly condensed version of a promotion letter; it includes the most important letter elements.

The section that follows discusses the basic considerations we deal with when writing a promotion letter—matters that were dealt with in the sample letter for Professor Whitehead.

Anatomy of a Typical Promotions Committee Letter

A promotion letter typically does the following, with varying degrees of detail and enthusiasm:

Nov. 5, 1995
To: Christopher Newman
             Chair, Conceptual Studies Program
From: V. I. Ulanov
             Chair, Promotions Committee
             Conceptual Studies Program

The Promotions Committee of the Conceptual Studies Program has voted unanimously to support the promotion of Alice South Whitehead from Assistant Professor to Associate Professor.

Professor Whitehead has published seventeen refereed articles (see attached) and two scholarly books, *Certainty, Love and Logic* (Harvard University Press, 1990) and *Signs and Significance* (Indiana University Press, 1993) that have received favorable reviews (see attached). One reviewer called her work "bold and imaginative," and another said her book on signs was a "pioneering effort that will help redefine cognitive studies."

We also have obtained several letters written on her behalf from scholars such as Jean-Marie Jean-Pierre of the CNRS in France, Bruno Blanco of the Cognitive Studies Institute of the University of Bologna, and Academician Ivan I. Ivanov of the University of Moscow's Neuroscience Institute.

In addition to her scholarly achievements, Professor Whitehead has contributed a great deal to the department, the college, and the university. She currently chairs the departmental curriculum committee and is also on the Dean search committee for the College of Cognitive Studies as well as the all-university General Education Committee.

Finally, Professor Whitehead has compiled an enviable teaching record. The data show that over the last five years, she has had an average of 1.19 in the student evaluations of her classes on a scale of 1 (highest) and 5 (lowest). We are attaching data that show her averages along with letters from students who have written on her behalf. A peer evaluation of her classroom teaching was extremely positive and described her teaching as "dynamic" and "remarkable." (See attached.)

The committee feels on the basis of the evidence cited above that Professor Whitehead is an outstanding scholar and teacher who strongly merits promotion to Associate Professor.

Figure 2.1. Promotion Letter

❶ *It opens with a statement about the committee's decision to support or not support a candidate for promotion.* If the vote was not unanimous, the figures are given for the vote. Sometimes, letters from professors who hold a minority position on the promotion (pro or con) are also sent to the dean.

❷ *It lists and evaluates the candidate's publications, quoting appraisals by others when possible.* It can discuss book reviews and letters from editors and mention whether the author's work is cited in articles and books.

❸ *It discusses other communication.* It can evaluate letters from colleagues in the same and other departments, letters from scholars at other institutions, letters from students, and so on about the candidate's teaching, collegiality, and service to the institution.

❹ *It evaluates the candidate's teaching skills.* Data are used from student evaluations taken over several years. Copies of memos by peer evaluators should also be included.

❺ *It says something about the candidate's service to the university and the department.* It discusses and evaluates the candidate's committee work for the department, school, and university; it is as specific as possible about committees the person has chaired, reports he or she has submitted, and so on.

❻ *It discusses the candidate's roles.* This discussion includes the candidate's current role in the department and what role he or she will play in the department's future plans in terms of topics such as curriculum and governance.

❼ *It describes the contributions of the candidate to the community at large.*

Dealing With Deficiencies in a Candidate

Generally speaking, academic institutions supply several specific criteria to be used in evaluating people for promotion, such as the items mentioned above, and say something about how these criteria are to be weighted. It makes sense to be honest and realistic, mentioning a candidate's deficiencies and weaknesses as well as strengths. This is a delicate matter and takes a good deal of finesse, because you do not want to be appear too negative about a candidate you are

1. Write in the active voice.
2. Write economically: Omit words you do not need.
3. Put your statements in a positive form.
4. Write directly. Avoid qualifiers when possible.
5. Be specific and concrete, not vague.
6. Keep related elements close to one another.
7. Write simply, avoiding stilted or jargon-filled language and overly complex sentences.
8. Structure your writing. Make an outline and follow it.
9. Write clearly. Avoid awkward and confusing constructions.
10. Use the appropriate tone. Avoid a breezy style, facetiousness, trite phrases, and too many figures of speech.

Figure 2.2. Rules for Effective Writing

supporting. It is generally impossible for a candidate to have high ratings in every area.

Where there are specific weaknesses, it is a good tactic to mention them, thereby strengthening your credibility and suggesting that you are being fair in your evaluation of the candidate. You then can assess the importance of the deficiencies and describe what, if anything, the candidate is doing to deal with them. You can also minimize them somewhat by focusing attention on the candidate's particular strengths and considering his or her special areas of expertise.

Rules for Writing Effective Letters

In *The Elements of Style*, a classic book on writing, William Strunk, Jr., and E. B. White discuss some of the most common stylistic errors and offer suggestions about how to avoid them and how to write better documents. Figure 2.2 synthesizes the most important points of Strunk and White's and other writing books and offers suggestions about how to write in an effective and stylish manner.

In the final analysis, writing involves using words and literary devices—such as alliteration, emphasis, balance, repetition, rhythm, and tone—to generate the effects and impressions you want and to call forth the responses you are seeking. You can break any rule as long as you achieve the effects and the results you want.

Remember that the letter you write on behalf of your candidate is the only opportunity you will have to influence the promotion process. Thus you owe it to your colleague to make as strong and convincing an argument as you can. This involves matters such as your letter's language (administrators and members of the university promotions committee will scrutinize the words you choose) and the case you build for your candidate. The very style of your letter—its language, its style, its polish—functions as a signifier of your support for the candidate.

The Components of Letters

Letters have specific features that are not found in memos: a return address, an inside address, a salutation, and a close. But the functions of a letter are the same: to communicate information to someone in a clear and unambiguous manner and to establish a paper trail, among other things. Figure 2.3 offers a typical letter in the "full block format" written by a textbook publisher to someone at an academic institution.

The letters we consider here—that is, formally written communications—have the following components:

A return address. In academic institutions the letterhead serves this purpose.

A date. This establishes when the letter was written.

An inside address. Here we name a person or group of people and give the address(es) at which this individual or group of people can be reached. This is generally positioned flush left.

ACME Publications	
115 John Locke Street	Return Address
Boston, MA	
Jan. 15, 1995	Date
Dr. David Hume, Ph.D.	
Department of Theoretical Concerns	Inside Address
North Central Metropolitan University	
Metropolitan City, California 94949	
Dear Dr. Hume:	Salutation

This is to inform you that we have received your manuscript, *An Enquiry Concerning Human Understanding* and have evaluated it. Although we find it interesting, and perhaps even provocative, we have not been able to think of a suitable market. It will not serve as a text in critical thinking courses or even in general philosophy courses, and the situation is such that we cannot publish books that will not have a large potential market. Perhaps you should try a university press.

We are returning the book to you and thank you for giving us the opportunity to consider it.

Sincerely yours,

Jacques Derrida-Barthes	Close
Acquisitions Editor	

Figure 2.3.

> *A salutation.* If the addressee holds a doctorate or has an academic position, that makes life easy: We can use the term "Dr." or the person's rank (e.g., "Assistant Professor"). If neither case applies and we know the marital status of a woman who is to receive our letters, then we write "Miss" or "Mrs."; however, if we do not know her marital status or if we know that she uses "Ms." in her letters, then we adopt this term. This also is usually positioned flush left.
>
> *The body of the letter.* The body conveys information, states why we are writing the letter and what actions we hope the person who receives the letter will take, and so on. It is a good strategy to (a) state conclusions before offering reasons, (b) make

requests before offering justifications, and (c) give answers to questions before offering explanations. Doing so helps the reader follow your chain of thinking better. You may also discuss events that have taken place, offer data of interest, or refer to other documents (memos, letters, reports, operational rules, etc.) in your letter. The body is typed single-spaced, with a line of white space between each paragraph, each of which starts flush left.

The close. Traditionally, we use a formal close such as "Yours truly" and "Sincerely yours." Only the first word is capitalized. This is also flush left.

The signature. The signature ordinarily includes our name, degree, and rank in the institution or our position; it is typed approximately four spaces below the close and flush left.

Other information. Beneath our name we put such matters as whether there are enclosures ("Enc.") or whether the letter is being sent to other people, in which case we name them (e.g., "cc.: Provost Jane Q. Public, Dean Z. Brontosaurus"). We indicate dictation (if any) by our initials and the initials of the person who typed the letter (e.g., "JD-B:pb").

Letter Formats

There are three common formats for letters:

1. *full block,* in which every element of the letter is flush left;
2. *regular block,* in which the return address, close, and signature are moved to the right; and
3. *semiblock,* in which the return address, close, and signature are moved to the right, and paragraphs are indented five spaces.

E-Mail and Faxes

E-Mail

The personal letter can be a remarkable literary creation, and the letters of great writers, artists, scientists, and politicians are often both superb creative works as well as important sources of information. Nowadays, the phone call and electronic mail ("E-mail") have grown in popularity as a form of direct communication or, more precisely, transmission. The letter, however, remains the most important form of written external communication.

E-mail is an extremely fast way to send information—memos, letters, and other documents—to others. You can reply to letters immediately and send documents to people all over the country (and world) without having to address an envelope or even type a return address. And your communication is transported in an instant.

But by its very nature, E-mail lends itself to being somewhat informal. You must be careful not to write too hastily: Once sent, E-mail cannot be retrieved and thrown in a wastebasket. Such transmission can happen easily if you are in a "chat" mode with someone.

So if you are communicating to someone and have to be careful about what you write, it is a good idea to avoid E-mail or, at the very least, write your document as a file, look it over, think carefully about it, and then send it. (E-mail is stored in backup files in university computers, so your E-mail correspondence is not as private as you might think; it can be accessed by others. The moral, then, is be doubly careful what you send by E-mail.)

E-mail writers often send copies to many other people. This can lead to a problem of clutter and information overload: E-mail is so convenient (perhaps even addictive) that people often find that they have 30 or 40 messages waiting for them when they turn on their computers to check their mail. Thus when sending E-mail, we must decide whether we should send copies of what we write to large numbers of our correspondents.

We also have to think about the length of the mail we send and make sure we do not write documents that are too long or that contain language or information that might embarrass ourselves or others.

Faxes

In addition to E-mail, we can now easily send a fax (short for "facsimile") transmission to someone almost anywhere in the world. Faxes are different from E-mail: Fax machines transmit already written and printed memos and letters; with E-mail we often write at the keyboard. It is common now for letterheads to contain both E-mail addresses and fax numbers.

Recently I had reason to write to someone at a university in Thailand. I sent an airmail letter and received a reply some 4 weeks later. The reply was written on stationery that gave a fax number. After that I was able to communicate with my correspondents in Thailand almost instantaneously.

Summary

In this chapter we have considered some of the most important aspects of writing letters of recommendation and dealt with a much more complicated kind of document: promotion letters. We also have covered such matters as letter formats, writing with style, E-mail, and faxes. Now we move on to our next subject: reports. Reports can be seen as extensions of memos and generally are written in memo formats, although they usually are much longer and often involve decisions made by committees that have been asked to undertake certain tasks related to an institution's operation.

3 | Writing Reports

A report is generally defined as *a formal account of the proceedings and conclusions of a person or members of some group of people charged with writing about an assigned topic of interest and concern*. Reports have a standard format, but often we find elements of a report included in a memo or a letter; the forms are often mixed together. A report is supposed to be objective and authoritative and recount the various aspects of what is being investigated in as truthful and fair a manner as possible.

The so-called *Rashomon* phenomenon (or how different parties to an event give different and contradictory accounts of what has transpired) makes us aware that it is often difficult to find out the truth about what happened when questioning witnesses and parties involved in incidents. There is also the matter of the way in which those who report on events interpret the evidence they get. So reports are not always accurate and objective.

Nevertheless, we can try to make our reports truthful, avoid being lied to by participants and witnesses involved in some incident, and avoid injecting partisan perspectives into our interpretation of the information we obtain.

The Problem With Reports

The problem with reports is that frequently they are like wolves in sheep's clothing. "Figures don't lie," the wits tell us, "but liars figure." What this suggests is that in conflict situations—whether caused by budget problems or different views of what should be done to deal with specific problems, people "use" data for their own purposes. They may produce reports full of objective data, but data, as we all know, can be selectively chosen and manipulated.

For example, many universities are having severe budget difficulties and are closing down departments and schools. These drastic steps are taken, we must assume, on the basis of reports made by committees that are charged with deciding which departments and schools are least necessary or least cost-effective relative to the mission of the university. These reports will be full of statistics about the number of students being serviced, the number of graduate students and quality of the graduate students in the department, the quality of the faculty, the ranking of the department or school by professional organizations, the ability of the university to absorb the tenured faculty members in other departments, and so on.

But in compiling statistics, a great deal of leeway is given in deciding which statistics are most important and should be included in the report and which are of secondary significance, or which aspects of an event should and should not be considered. As anyone who has compiled and used data can tell you, it is not obtaining data that causes the most difficulties, generally speaking, but how they are interpreted.

The report frequently is something that is used to provide cover. For example, if the president of a university wants to close down the library school or eliminate the sociology department and some faculty or administrative committee's report recommends that the library or department be maintained, then the president might reject the report as flawed. If the report recommends the library school be closed down or the sociology department eliminated, then the president can do so, arguing that although the decision was hard to make and one he regrets a great deal, he was convinced to do so by the report.

Reports then are often pseudo-objective "sheep's clothing" covering the "wolf" of academic politics and personal passions. And it is because most people who have been around academic institutions for any length of time know this that reports are often extremely controversial and seldom accepted on face value, especially by those who might be harmed if the recommendations of the reports were to be implemented. Thus reports must be seen as political documents and, because lawyers have insinuated themselves into our lives nowadays, as documents that may ultimately be used in legal proceedings. Although this is particularly true of reports, we can say the same about every document we write in academic settings.

Suggestions for Writing Reports

What follows is a list of things to keep in mind when writing reports (and, by extension, any kind of document used in academic organizations).

❶ *Write in a formal, reserved manner.* Reports are not written in a conversational style or a breezy style that suggests a lack of seriousness or a casual approach toward affairs. Avoid making snide comments and showing how clever you are.

Example: This report is offered by the General Studies Review Committee, which was charged with examining and evaluating the current General Studies Curriculum and offering suggestions for changes to improve the quality of the General Studies Curriculum, the way it is implemented, and related matters.

Example: The Budget Committee is outraged over the way funds are allocated among the departments. Dean Newton has given the Physics Department a ridiculous amount of money even though it has hardly any students and has taken desperately needed money away from other departments in the school of physical sciences.

versus

Example: The figures below suggest that budget allocations should be reviewed and adjusted to better represent the distribution of students in the various departments of the school. For example, the Physics Department, with 20 percent of the students in the school, gets 38 percent of the budget, while the Chemistry Department, with 40 percent of the students, receives only 30 percent of the budget.

Department	Students (%)	Budget (%)
Physics	20	38
Chemistry	40	30
Biological Sciences	22	16
Physical Sciences	18	16

Figure 3.1.

This statement is very direct. It tells who authored the report and what the committee's charge was. It avoids snide comments (such as suggesting that the General Studies Curriculum is a "disaster area" and "in a state of chaos") and adopts a serious and matter-of-fact tone.

❷ *Do not use emotionally charged language.* The report is supposed to be objective and reasoned. If you use emotional terms, if there are insults and expressions of feeling, your credibility will be undermined. If you wish to put an emotional charge in your writing, then quote statistics and other information that pack an emotional charge. Let the facts do the shouting; to put it another way, "Show, don't tell." (For an example, see Figure 3.1.)

❸ *Offer evidence to support conclusions that a reasonable person could accept.* Whenever there are disputes or matters at issue, both sides usually have reasons to support their positions. The question of who is right (if that can be answered) often boils down to a matter of whose evidence seems most compelling.

The table in Figure 3.1 offers data on the percentage of students in each department in the school of science and the percentage of budget allocations for each department. The table shows that the distribution of money for departments is skewed in favor of Physics, while Chemistry gets less than what would seem to be its fair share. There may be reasons for this, which can justify the situation, but the chart offers a good overview of how the money is actually being spent and puts the burden on the dean to justify the way the money is being allocated.

❹ *Explain your decision-making processes in detail.* It is useful to describe how you came about making your decisions: what evidence seemed most pertinent, what factors were most important, whose position seemed most correct. If you do not describe how you arrived at your position, then others will spend a good deal of time trying to figure it out and challenging the way in which you arrived at your position. (Even if you do explain your decision making, people will try to figure out why you "really" made your decisions: Were there political factors of consequence? Do you harbor a grudge? Are personal friendships of consequence?)

❺ *Be as specific as you can.* In writing your reports, try to maintain focus and avoid making generalizations that go beyond the data you have collected. Do not leave yourself (and your fellow report writers) open to attack. Use factual material, statistical data, quotations from interested parties, and suggestions from experts to make your case. It is often a good idea to deal with both the positive and negative aspects of, say, a proposed policy change to show that you are fair and reasonable. Generic comments such as "A creative response to this problem is needed" or "Something must be done about this serious matter" are weak and ineffectual. Be more specific.

> **Example:** During the past three years, 51% of the students in the freshman class transferred to other schools. We suggest the following steps be taken to lower this figure. First, survey the complaints made by freshman students and see what suggestions they have to offer. Second, investigate policies used at other institutions that have been effective in dealing with this problem.

It is much better to avoid platitudes and generalizations and offer specific steps that might be taken to alleviate problems.

❻ *Learn to qualify assertions and be judicious.* It is often a good idea to avoid direct assertions and to qualify suggestions. The aim is to soften the impact of the recommendations and to suggest that suggested actions are taken on the basis of necessity, not desire.

❼ *Never put anything in writing that could be used against you in any way.* You must always assume that whatever you write might be leaked by someone or might be discovered by someone and then made known. So-called confidential reports and other documents may not really be confidential. This includes memos, letters, notes, and files on computer disks. Remember, if it is in writing, it can and might be used against you.

A Sample Report

I recently received a report that, with its attachments, was more than 20 pages long. What I offer here is a highly condensed version of a report that covers many of the topics that are found in conventional reports. The report in Figure 3.2 is modeled on one created by a committee at San Francisco State University.

The example in Figure 3.2 has the basic components of a report. The executive summary tells who charged the task force (the provost) and what its mission was. The body of the report tells how the task force operated: what it did, how it obtained input from the faculty, and its use of experts. The recommendations by the task force are very specific and detailed. The summary of findings reaffirms the decision of the task force, discusses the benefits of having the proposed center, and suggests when it should be established. Finally, in the appendix, a series of attachments is offered that includes the task force membership, letters from faculty members at the institution about the proposed teaching center, what other institutions have teaching centers and how they operate, and suggestions about how the center will function.

Report of the Task Force on Teaching Enhancement

Summary. At the request of Provost A. Tchitchikov, an all-university committee, the Task Force on Teaching Enhancement, was formed to investigate the feasibility of setting up a center to enhance teaching here at Northwest Central Metropolitan University. After soliciting input from students and colleagues and investigating what has been done at other institutions, the Task Force unanimously recommends that a Center for the Enhancement of University Teaching be established.

Body of the Report. The Task Force met on a monthly basis, and members of the Task Force also participated in a weekend retreat. Members attended several conferences dealing with teaching at the college level and invited several experts on the subject to address it. The Task Force also solicited comments from the faculty by sending letters out and putting an advertisement in the campus newspaper. We received numerous replies, most of which were supportive and positive. Several subcommittees were formed to investigate how a center might be funded, how it would function, and who would direct it.

Recommendations. It was decided that: ONE, the Center should be seen as a faculty resource that would help teachers develop their teaching skills and be shielded from retention and tenure considerations; TWO, it should be housed on campus and be readily accessible to all faculty members; and THREE, it should have assigned time of 60 percent for its director, 40 percent for an assistant director, a full-time secretary, and adequate funds for computers, stationery, and other needed supplies.

Summary of the Findings. The committee recommends that this Center be established by the end of the current academic year, despite the current budgetary problems; the committee believes this center will greatly enhance the quality of instruction on this campus.

Appendix. (1) The charge to the Task Force, (2) a list of Task Force members, (3) faculty letters, (4) a report on teaching centers at other institutions, and (5) suggestions about how the proposed Teaching Center will operate.

Figure 3.2.

The Parts of a Report

Reports usually include the following items, although shorter reports often combine some of these elements: (a) memo or letter of transmission, (b) cover, (c) title page, (d) preface, (e) table of contents, (f) list of tables and illustrations, (g) acknowledgments, (h) executive summary, (i) body of the report, (j) recommendations, (k) summary of findings, (l) appendixes, and (m) bibliography and references.

We will now consider the main parts of the typical report in more detail.

❶ *Memo or letter of transmission.* This letter informs the reader that a report on a given subject is to follow; it may include material on why the report was commissioned (the charge to the committee) and who wrote the report. It also frequently contains a list of the members of the committee and subcommittees that generated the report and their signatures.

❷ *Table of contents.* This lists the parts of the report so that the reader can see quickly what is in the report. Make sure that the titles of the various sections are descriptive.

❸ *List of tables and illustrations.* This enables the reader to see what kind of supporting information is used and to find data more quickly.

❹ *Acknowledgments.* Here the writer thanks those who helped create the report.

❺ *Executive summary.* When writing reports and when doing most writing for organizations, we state our findings or conclusions (or main points) at the beginning of our communication. This enables the reader to see immediately the point of our communication and to follow our argument better. This summary is the moral equivalent of a thesis statement or an abstract. It should be relatively short.

❻ *Body of the report.* Here we cover the basic elements found in all reports: who, what, where, when, why, and how.

Who is involved in the matter being reported on?

What happened?

Where did it happen?

When did it take place?

Why is the matter of concern?

How did it happen?

In dealing with these matters, we often need to go into considerable detail, and different sections of the report will have different lengths, depending on the situation on which we are reporting. Depending on the complexity of the topic being investigated, reports can vary from just a few pages in length to very substantial, reaching 50 or 100 pages.

The longer the report, the less likely that people will read it all the way through or carefully—unless it has implications for individuals or departments, in which case it will be scrutinized in great detail and probably engender numerous memos from not only those who like what it says, but also, and in particular, those who do not.

❼ *Recommendations.* The report ultimately leads to some recommendations—about a course of action to be pursued, a policy to be implemented, and so on.

❽ *Appendixes.* Here we supply any data or other factual material used in the report. This also includes a bibliography and references when relevant.

When in Doubt, Leave It Out!

If you are not sure about something, do not use it in your report. On the other hand, material you write may be of use in the future to show that you and your colleagues suggested some policy, had some idea, and so on, so a corollary to the "when in doubt" rule is "If it might be useful to have it on the record, write it down." When you write things down, you can show that you did certain things or had certain ideas at a given point in time, and this material might be of help to you if your reputation is attacked or there are problems about copyright matters or the development (and maybe even the "ownership") of ideas. It also helps to write down ideas that you may want to work on at some later date or that others might find useful in tracing the evolution of ideas or, and one never knows, your career. The written word lives, and in academic life, most of us live by the written word.

Conclusions

Reports need not be dull and boring. Even though there is a prescribed format for reports, that does not mean that they cannot be lively, interesting, challenging, and perhaps even exciting. When reports are boring, it is generally because they are written in a bureaucratic, abstract manner, using a style we might call "Latinate officialese." It is not that the subject matter is intrinsically boring but that the authors of reports write in a boring style.

In *On Writing Well,* William Zinsser states:

> But just because people work for an institution they don't have to write like one. Institutions can be warmed up. Administrators and executives can be turned into human beings. Information can be imparted clearly and without pomposity. It's a question of remembering that readers identify with people, not with abstractions like "profitability," or with Latinate nouns like "utilization" and "implementation," or with inert constructions in which nobody can be visualized doing something ("prefeasibility studies are in the paperwork stage"). (1985, pp. 145-146)

Zinsser's chapter on "Professional Writing and Business Writing" is worth reading along with the chapter on writing reports in Neil J. Smelser's book in this series, *Effective Committee Service.*

Summary

This chapter has discussed the basic elements of reports and dealt with what we can do to make these documents more readable, interesting, and authoritative. We now move on to the last of our basic types of documents—proposals— and their basic elements and, of particular importance, how to write proposals that work. By "work," I mean proposals that are persuasive, that use a variety of appeals to convince decision makers to support and, when money is involved, fund them.

4 | Proposals That Work

Proposals are documents that attempt to persuade someone to do something—with the implication that the suggested course of action is in everyone's best interest. The proposal may involve suggestions for changing the general education policies of the university, requesting funds to purchase new equipment, or for a leave of absence for a faculty member to do research—the list could go on indefinitely. Needs and desires are infinite, but funds, alas, are finite. This chapter, then, deals with the way in which proposals should be organized and with the art of persuasion. (Book proposals and grant proposals will be covered by other books in this series.)

Proposal Design

There is no single way to organize a proposal, but the basic components of proposals are, generally speaking, as follow:

1. An *introduction* gives an overview or background and sets the stage for the most important section of the proposal, the body of the proposal.
2. A *body* supplies the details of what is proposed and the justification for the proposal.
3. A *conclusion* urges that the proposal be accepted.

33

4. A *budget* shows how any funds needed to implement the proposal will be spent.
5. *Documentation* supports the body of the proposal.

We will now consider each section in more detail, starting with the proposal's introduction.

Introduction to the Proposal

The introduction gives the reader a general overview of the situation to which the proposal relates, offers background material of interest, and sets the stage for the main part of the proposal, its body. The introduction should not be slighted: It can whet the reader's interest and establish the sense that the proposal is of some consequence.

Body of the Proposal

The body more or less makes the case for supporting the proposal and deals with several elemental matters, including the most common ones below.

Qualifications of Those Making the Proposal

A qualifications section shows that the people involved in the proposal have the requisite knowledge and experience to do what is desired if the proposal is approved. For example, one might offer material on the individuals' teaching histories as well as lists of relevant publications and information about their work in the field. This might involve a description of other projects they have previously completed and the results of their work.

If the proposal deals with modifying the general education program, for example, it would make sense that the people making the proposal should have experience teaching general education courses, have done research on general education, or have some other connection with the matter such as involvement with general education at the policy level.

Substance of the Proposal

The proposal is actually made in the body. Here you describe *why* what you want to do is important, explain in some detail *what* you will do, and discuss what *results* you expect from implementing your proposal. You cite data and use other materials that support your proposal, such as interviews with interested parties.

Remember, you must convince someone or some group of people to do something—give you and your colleagues funds, make changes in the curriculum, change some policy, and so on. You should also attach, at the end of your report, a section with supporting documentation that is more complete than the materials you use in this section of the proposal.

Let us return to the topic of general education, a subject of endless controversy among academics. You might suggest that the current general education program be scrapped and that a new system based on this or that theory be put into place. You would need to detail the courses that would qualify as general education courses, the means by which students would select these courses, and the number of credits of general education courses that students would be required to take, among many other concerns.

Benefits of Accepting the Proposal

The proposal's benefits are the heart of the matter. A written proposal should show how its adoption will have specific benefits or payoffs for your department, school, or university. This is the "sales" part of the proposal. It also is a good tactic to deal with the costs involved in not accepting the proposal when it involves such actions as obtaining new equipment, changing elements of the curriculum, and so on. The argument generally is that it is cost-effective to accept the proposal and that short-term expenditures will lead to long-term savings and improvements.

It is useful here to take another look at the proposal about making changes in the general education program. Your proposal would have to show how the new program would be an improvement over the old one: how it would advance the education of students, make them aware of the "best that's been thought and said," better prepare them for doing work in their majors, help them become more responsible citizens, and give them an appreciation of history, philosophy, the sciences, the social sciences, and the arts.

A Plan of Execution

This section deals with how the proposal will be implemented: what will be done, in what order, and why. The size and scope of this section will depend on the complexity of the proposal. Here you can offer a projected time schedule, showing how the proposal will be implemented in general and at what points the various stages of the proposal occur.

An Itemized Budget

In cases where funds are requested, the budget will show the decision makers what the costs are and how the proposal can actually be implemented for the amount of money requested. After this, it is a good idea to reiterate the matter's importance and to request rapid approval of the proposal for all of its stated reasons.

Documentation

The documentation section offers data and other relevant materials in support of the proposal. This section contains more complete data and other materials than is used in the proposal's body. For example, in the case of suggested changes in the general education plan, statistics might show how students feel about the current general education plan, memos and letters from faculty members might show their difficulties in advising students about the current general education program, and information from other institutions might show how they have modified their general education programs along the lines that are suggested in the proposal.

Persuasive Writing

Several methods can be used in persuading people to accept your proposals. We must assume a "built-in" resistance by those who evaluate proposals, based on receiving numerous proposals, all of which argue that they should be implemented or funded. What this text offers is a microcourse in rhetoric, which is defined by Aristotle in his *Rhetoric* as "the faculty of observing in any given case the available means of persuasion." He explains:

> Of the modes of persuasion furnished by the spoken word there are three kinds. The first kind depends on the personal character of the speaker; the second on putting the audience into a certain frame of mind; the third on the proof, or apparent proof, provided by the words of the speech itself.

He later adds that "a statement is persuasive because it is directly self-evident or because it appears to be proved from other statements that are so. In either case, it is persuasive because there is somebody whom it persuades." That somebody is the key to the situation. It is not a bad idea for anyone interested in persuasion to read Aristotle, but here I offer suggestions for persuading a "somebody" to accept your proposal.

❶ *Appeal to self-interest.* Show that accepting a given proposal is in the self-interest of all the parties involved, because of the various benefits that will come with the proposal's implementation.

❷ *Anticipate objections to the proposal.* Here you anticipate objections that might be raised about your proposal and show that they are not correct. You are conducting an argument about your proposal, and, because you are doing the writing, you can make sure that your side seems the most persuasive.

❸ *Use your reader's ideas and beliefs to your advantage.* In other words, work to strike a responsive chord and build your argument on the preconceptions, beliefs, values, attitudes, and so on of the person evaluating your proposal. Learn what your grantor wants before you submit your proposal; you may even find it most persuasive.

❹ *Deal with short-term or long-term (or both) benefits.* Depending on the situation and the nature of your proposal, focus on the long-term benefits if the short-term cost will be great or if the impact seems of minor consequence (or vice versa). Or deal with both aspects, if that is the best way to support your proposal.

❺ *Show how your proposal is cost-efficient.* Even though it may cost money to implement your proposal, if you can show that it is cost-efficient, has a payoff, will greatly improve the quality of the instruction or the research, or will lead to increased savings, then your proposal will have a greater chance of being accepted.

❻ *Adopt a confident tone.* In your writing style, assume that the value of your proposal is obvious and self-evident, and so write in a confident manner. But do not overdo it and antagonize your reader.

❼ *Suggest that of all possible solutions to a problem, your proposal offers the best solution.* There are often many different courses of action to be taken to deal with some problem or issue. If you can show that your particular solution is better than all others suggested, then you will have a much better chance of getting your proposal accepted and, if money is involved, funded.

❽ *Show how other proposals are self-contradictory.* If you can show that competing proposals are, in reality, inconsistent and self-contradictory, then you will have an extremely strong position, because nobody can be on both sides of an argument and still be correct. This is a sanitized version of so-called negative campaigning.

❾ *Appeal to emotions in a subtle manner.* We know from advertising that people are swayed by emotional appeals, but in proposals these appeals must be carefully disguised. The focus must be on such aspects as the prestige to be gained by the department, school, or university by having a new computer laboratory or whatever, and how funding the proposal will demonstrate that the decision maker is a visionary, a bold thinker, and will reflect positively on all involved. If you can suggest that adopting the proposal might gain the school and the president national recognition and so on, then so much the better.

A Final Note

Writing good proposals is an art that makes use of another art, persuasion. We must always consider the human equation when writing, because proposals are not always evaluated strictly on the basis of logic and the quality of the argument that is made. Friendships, grudges, psychological problems, moods, and prestige are also factors that influence the way people evaluate proposals; they influence all aspects of life in universities and other complex organizations.

But despite these matters, a strongly written proposal carries an enormous amount of weight and can overcome resistance. That is what proposal writing is all about. Persuading means winning people over to your point of view, convincing people to accept your proposal by making a powerful argument—one that appeals to people's emotions as well as their reason. When you make your proposal, therefore, be sure you put enough emphasis on the means you use to persuade decision makers to accept it.

Summary

In this chapter we have considered how to write proposals that "work"—that is, we discussed methods that can be used to convince administrators and others who evaluate and fund proposals to accept and, when money is involved, to fund your proposal. We have also examined the various elements generally found in proposals. Proposals can vary in length from a few pages to book-length documents, depending on the complexity of the matter under consideration. They need to be convincing and they need to be readable—the next subject to be discussed. Making documents more readable involves such tasks as varying the lengths of sentences and paragraphs, showing the logical structure of the document, and using lists and subheads to organize and display ideas.

PART II

Writing Effective Business Documents

5 | Readable Writing

We can write reports that are full of important information and we can make proposals that could, if adopted, lead to truly significant improvements in the curriculum or some other aspect of our institutions, but if people do not read the documents we write, then our time and energy have been wasted. One way or another, we must find a way to maximize the readability of the documents we write. We have to find ways to make our documents interesting, and, if possible, easy—even pleasurable—for people to read.

Making Documents Readable

We can do many things to make our documents more readable. Remember, of course, that we always adopt a style of writing that is suited for the people who will read our documents. When we write in academic institutions, we generally write in a formal, nonconversational, and reserved manner. But this does not mean we cannot have character in our writing.

What follows is a list to consider when writing memos and other documents.

❶ *Mix up your sentence lengths and avoid long, convoluted sentences.* It is easier to read short (or relatively short) sentences than long ones. But if you only use short sentences, then you will bore your readers, because we like variety. On the other hand, avoid—to the extent you can—long, highly complex sentences that are hard to follow.

Brand Blanchard discusses this matter in his book *On Philosophical Style* (1954). He writes:

> [E]ach sentence should carry the thought one step forward. But what is to count as one step? A sentence at its simplest makes one statement, but if we were to make only one statement per sentence, our writing would be unbearable. "Sir John came out of his house. He wore a top hat. He wore a monocle. He wore spats. He carried a cane. He hailed a taxi." Intolerable! When details all hang together to make one picture, they can be grasped without difficulty as forming a single unit, and we throw them together in one sentence: "Sir John, radiant in morning dress, with top hat, monocle, spats, and cane, emerged from his door and hailed a taxi." But in regions of difficulty, it is a test of literary skill to know and to take into account the length of the reader's stride. The ideal is a row of stepping-stones just far enough apart to enable him to keep moving without compelling him to make hops, skips, and jumps, still less leaps in the dark. (pp. 51-52)

Short sentences, one after the other, distract us and we find ourselves, almost against our will, involved with the form of the sentences rather than their content. Primer-style writing also bores and insults us by writing as if we were children. We want to use different lengths in our sentences to develop a rhythm that readers will find complex, challenging, and pleasing.

❷ *Mix up the lengths of your paragraphs and avoid very short or extremely long paragraphs.* Generally speaking, a paragraph is devoted to one basic idea. The average paragraph, so the grammar books tell us, should run between 75 and 150 words, but some paragraphs can be shorter and others longer, depending on their function. For example, some paragraphs serve as transitions and can be short; in other cases, a short paragraph can highlight an idea. In each paragraph you should take some central concept or topic and develop it by using examples, discussing implications, giving details, offering reasons for things, and defining terms.

If, on the other hand, you have nothing but extremely long paragraphs, you will also tire your readers. You will bore them because they seek variety in paragraph length and will cause difficulties for them because you will, most probably, be providing too much detail and discussion and the readers will get lost, unable to figure out what is important and what is unimportant.

❸ *Vary your focus between the concrete and the general.* When you write documents, move up and down on what semanticists call the "ladder of abstraction." For example, in a report about general education, move back and forth from discussions of what students say about these specific courses to discussions of issues relating to the curriculum in some department or school or broader discussions of the curriculum in general. Or you can write about a student, Jane Q. Student, who would be at the lowest rung of the ladder of abstraction, or about the highest rung—humanity—and many levels in between.

If you only deal with one level, you will tire your readers. And you will also face the problem of either not being able to generalize very well (if you just write about Jane Q. Student) or only being able to generalize and not deal with specifics (if you write only about humanity). Philosophers tend to write in a very general and broad manner that is high on the ladder of abstraction, which is why they are often so difficult to read. Readable writing moves up and down this ladder; by doing so, it creates variety and generates reader interest.

❹ *Make your logical structure show in the document as you progress from point to point and use transitions.* It is a good idea to help readers see the structure of your argument by giving them occasional cues so they know where they were, where they are, and where they are going. You can do this by making frequent use of transitions, which are grammatical devices that help your readers anticipate what is to come and see how you are developing your ideas. Transitions make your writing more fluid, more coherent. Transitions help readers follow the course of an argument. You do not want to use them mechanically, but you must offer enough transitions to make things as easy as possible for readers.

Besides using transitions, you can offer a paragraph that outlines the topics you will be dealing with and, at strategic points, you can offer summary statements that tell your reader what you have done so far and what you will be doing next.

❺ *Use lists to organize ideas and points you wish to make.* In addition to using transitions and summaries, you can also list points you are making by using numbers or the words *first, second, third,* and so on. But be sure your writing becomes more than a fleshed-out list of points to be made. That becomes very tedious. If you use lists, make sure that you have enough descriptive and explanatory matter and examples to offset the mechanical nature of the list process.

❻ *Use subheads to set ideas off, give them visual display, and guide your reader from topic to topic.* You can use subheads to show readers what aspect you are dealing with of your general topic. Subheads are, more or less, outlining devices that show what you are going to discuss; they also break up the text and provide a bit of visual relief for readers. Solid blocks of text are intimidating; if you can break them up with subheads and "infographics" (charts, graphs, and other visual displays of information), your document will seem less formidable to your readers.

This book makes use of several of these devices. For example, this chapter could have been written without subheads (typographically setting off its main points), but that would have made my argument much more difficult to follow. You will find not only subheads in this book, but also different typefaces to distinguish certain more important material from the regular text. In addition, various lists and charts function as infographics.

Somehow you must find a way to make your organization show but without letting it overwhelm your writing. You have to be judicious about using lists, charts, transitions, subheads, and other organizational devices, but you need them to help your reader negotiate your document.

❼ *Avoid jargon and technological terms as much as possible.* In some cases, of course, it is necessary to deal with highly technical matters that are best understood by specialized vocabulary. When you do so (for example, if you are requesting devices to be used in science laboratories), you must explain the terms you use and make sure your reader, who may be from a different discipline, will understand what you are discussing.

George Orwell offered a wonderful spoof of bureaucratic writing. First, he quotes from Ecclesiastes:

I returned and saw under the sun, that the race is not to the swift, nor the battle to the strong, neither yet bread to the wise, nor yet riches to men of understanding, nor yet favor to men of skill; but time and chance happeneth to them all.

Orwell then renders the same passage in bureaucratic language:

Objective consideration of contemporary phenomena compels the conclusion that success or failure in competitive activities exhibits no tendency to be commensurate with innate capacity, but that a considerable element of the unpredictable must invariably be taken into account.

This abstract and jargon-filled rendering is typical of what we too often find in material written in academic institutions: long words, ponderous thoughts, no rhythm or bite, no vitality, and no detail or images that capture the imagination.

❽ *Do not use abbreviations.* You may know what an abbreviation stands for, but others may not. Certainly some organizations are identified by acronyms—such as NATO and UNESCO. If you use an acronym, first spell out the subject's full name so that your reader knows what the acronym means.

❾ *Search for the exact word.* The French have a phrase, "le mot juste" ("the exact word"), that suggests that in certain places in our documents there is one—and only one—word that will do, only one word that captures the essence of things. We should always try to find that "exact" word, because its shadings, its implications, its color profoundly affect the way our readers will respond to our writing.

❿ *Use figurative language, examples, comparisons, and other descriptive devices.* When you write, it is sometimes a good idea to use analogies to help your readers visualize what you are discussing. And it is also helpful to support generalizations with concrete examples, case studies that are similar and instructive, and data that are relevant.

Perhaps the best way to think about language is to assume that *every* word makes a difference. Writing can be looked on—and this is admittedly somewhat reductionist—as a way of creating impressions in people, of generating effects with intention; it is through words that writers achieve their goals.

It may be a memo to convince the dean to fund a new computer laboratory or to convince the provost to promote one of your colleagues. Whatever the case, in memos, letters, reports, and proposals it is the words that count and do the work. And each word has a particular effect, gives your thoughts a specific coloration, and will be interpreted by readers in certain ways.

In much writing in academic institutions (and elsewhere as well), certain code words are used to say one thing and suggest something else. Take the matter of letters of recommendation. These codes are used because in some cases the people we write about are given copies of what we write about them or, as the result of a grievance procedure or lawsuit, gain access to them. I have dealt with these code words elsewhere, but keep in mind that in many cases people will not only read, but also scrutinize every word you have used in some document, which means you must be extremely careful about what you say and how you say it.

You must do whatever you can to make your document readable. You must learn to write clearly, to write with style, to give your document an element of personality, and to have it somehow reflect your "voice," even though you must keep yourself in the background. I take liberties here with a facetious statement about a writer to make a final point: "His prose was purple, but his books were read." Your prose should not be purple, but do whatever you can to make sure that your memos and other documents are read.

Summary

This chapter discussed various strategies for writing more readable documents. Among the topics dealt with were making the logical structure of documents show, varying sentence and paragraph lengths, moving up and down the ladder of abstraction, and avoiding jargon and bureaucratese. We move to a discussion of two related topics: how to use brainstorming to generate creative writing ideas and how to do collaborative writing.

6 | Developing Creative Ideas

Brainstorming is an idea-generating technique that can be used in both the planning and writing of documents. It is used in so-called think tanks and in advertising agencies; its use also is well suited to academic problem solving. The most important aspect of brainstorming is in thinking up ideas as fast as possible without censorship of any kind. Every idea mentioned is noted, and no ideas are dismissed as ridiculous, silly, far out, or crazy. Groups sometimes produce a synergy as members inspire, motivate, and encourage one another; the result can be an enormous number of ideas.

You need ideas when you both develop and implement a writing plan, and brainstorming is a useful way of getting them. You generally get more ideas than you need, and many of them will be ridiculous or useless, but it's better to have more than you need than not enough. Ideas can be generated in other ways, of course. Once you know your writing topic or problem, you can do research to find others' ideas and solutions for similar circumstances.

Thus brainstorming is a very powerful way of coming up with ideas to deal with everything from revising your department's curriculum to outmaneuvering some antagonistic individual or department with whom you or your department are in conflict. Departmental and committee discussions occasionally take on surreal qualities and become very much like brainstorming sessions, so the line between discussion and brainstorming sometimes is hard to draw.

How Brainstorming Works

How brainstorming works exactly is hard to say, but it probably functions by allowing the creative elements of the psyche free play. It would seem to be a "right brain" activity —that is, one in which the creative and holistic aspects of the mind are dominant and "left brain" activities involving logic and rationality are less important and so momentarily suppressed or turned off.

Brainstorming groups are sometimes composed of people who have widely different areas of expertise. An executive from a think tank once told me about the composition of his typical brainstorming groups: artists, psychologists, physicists, engineers, business executives, athletes, and so on. The idea is to bring together a variety of different people and set them to work on some topic or problem to see what "wild ideas" they might come up with that might lead to solutions to problems or to new products.

How to Conduct a Brainstorming Session With a Group

The rules of brainstorming in groups are relatively simple, but they must be strictly followed.

❶ *A group small enough to interact with one another must be assembled in a room that is conducive to this activity.* The space should be small enough that members of the group are not too distant from one another. The door should be locked to prevent interruptions. It is a good idea to make food and beverages available to the members of the group so no one is distracted by hunger pangs.

In my department, for example, we occasionally schedule "re-treats" in which we use brainstorming to deal with everything from problems we have with administrators to figuring out what to call ourselves and what we can do to prepare our department and our students for the future.

❷ *The basic rule of brainstorming is that no ideas are to be rejected for any reason.* The session can be tape-recorded so that no ideas are lost, but in general having someone take notes is all that is needed. Some-one should be designated as facilitator—someone who can be non-judgmental and who can foster an atmosphere of openness to all ideas, no matter how ridiculous they may seem. A sense of humor helps.

This process is very similar to the "talking cure" in psychother-apy, which assumes that if patients talk about whatever comes to mind, important material will be revealed that will help therapists make astute diagnoses and thus indicate how patients can be "cured" of their afflictions or at least helped with them.

❸ *Because ideas tend to generate other ideas, facilitators should encour-age other members of the group to play around with ideas as they are offered.* Brainstorming assumes that ideas from one person can be used to suggest other ideas to group members. The more ideas generated, the better. And the wilder and the crazier the ideas, the better.

In some respects, brainstorming is similar to dreaming. In our dreams, using processes that are not immediately accessible to our conscious mind, we sometimes solve problems whose solutions evaded us when we worked on them in a waking state. Some problems are solved creatively, using resources buried in our psyches and un-conscious minds, areas over which we have little or no direct control.

❹ *After the brainstorming session ends, a different process begins.* The ideas generated must be examined in terms of their potentialities and possibilities. One principal reason for brainstorming is to dis-cover new ideas. Another reason is to uncover ideas we did not know we had, but which once revealed might be extremely useful. We might brainstorm, for example, to get ideas to justify our deci-sion to revise the department's curriculum and make changes in the content and number of required courses or to find reasons to sup-port our request for funds for a computer laboratory. The ideas we get from brainstorming should be incorporated later into the docu-ments we write.

Using the ideas generated by the brainstorming team is done after the brainstorming session has concluded. It is not the primary or immediate task of the brainstorming group, although once the session is finished, the members can review the various ideas generated and offer suggestions about each idea's potential.

We brainstorm because some problems we face do not seem to have decent or apparent solutions (and we hope brainstorming will help us find something we did not think of, perhaps magically pulling something out of a hat) or because the seemingly logical solutions to problems we face do not strike us as very good. For our purposes, brainstorming is always a means to an end: creating an effective document.

Brainstorming and Organizing Ideas

Distinguishing between brainstorming and outlining ideas is difficult in many cases. The latter technique suggests that writers know more or less what they will be writing about and are trying to establish the best way to organize their material. Brainstorming suggests that one is looking for ideas and topics to write about. It is more of a process of discovery. Maybe the best way to think about these to processes is to say that they can overlap: The linearity and logical aspects of outlining can be combined with the idea-creating and idea-generating qualities of brainstorming.

When you start writing from an outline you often discover that the process of writing often generates new ideas and that the words you use sometimes take on a power of their own and shape the document you are writing. The act of writing is, after all, a creative process, one that often has its own imperatives. But you must have something to start with, ideas to get you going, information that you wish to write about. And brainstorming followed by selecting ideas from the session for use in an outline is a very good way to get started with any writing project, whether it be a committee report or a journal article.

Collaborative Writing

I often divide my writing classes into groups of three students and give them short team-writing assignments to do in class. These sessions frequently produce an incredible amount of group energy and enthusiasm, and the students laugh a great deal. They frequently stimulate ideas in one another, so much can be gained from this kind of writing.

But students sometimes mention problems that develop from uncooperative students who refuse to become team players. Some students must have things their way or they will not work with the team. Other students who are shy or lack confidence seem to play no role in their groups: They simply sit and listen to the other two students, who do all of the talking and writing. Cultural differences might play a role here. Despite the potential problems of this team form of collaborative writing, considerable benefits can be gained if the technique can be used successfully.

Collaborative Writing in the Academic World

A great deal of writing that is done in the business and professional world is collaborative, with people working together to produce documents, whether as memos, promotion letters, or job advertisements. (Approximately 60% of all writing in the business world is done in teams.) This team-written document may then be reviewed, edited, and revised by other people in superior positions as it moves toward acceptance and reproduction. To explain why collaborative writing is so common and to help facilitate this kind of writing, we will deal with both the reasons for using collaborative writing and its methods.

Reasons for Collaborative Writing

Organizational studies have shown that people often work better and more efficiently in teams because of a kind of frequently occurring dynamic. As individual team members stimulate ideas in and bond and establish personal rapport with one another, they also energize the others. In fact, sometimes it is more efficient for projects to be handed to teams than to leave them to individuals. Team members may have special competence and expertise in certain areas that will expedite the creation of documents. They can provide ideas and suggestions when the document is being planned or outlined. Or when time is a factor, a team can divide a project into parts, parceling them out to individuals and then assembling them either collectively or through assignment to an individual or a smaller team.

For example, if a department has a five-year review to write for the administration, the task might be sensibly divided up and given to department members who teach specific areas; they would each write a short report that dealt with his or her area and answer certain questions that the departmental review must consider. These sectional reports, which also might be written by small teams of department members, can then be assembled into a final departmental review.

Methods of Collaborative Writing

Three specific collaborative-writing techniques are described below.

The Team Draft

In the team draft method, a document is created collectively in one or more work sessions. Group dynamics are most actively at play, both positively and negatively, within these sessions. In other words, it is when the whole group works together to generate a document that differences in beliefs, attitudes, and personality types become most evident. Some kind of accord must be reached and some group members have to restrain themselves and one another, so no one member dominates. The benefit of this technique is that members of these dynamic groups often spark valuable ideas in one another.

Divide and Conquer

In the divide-and-conquer method, a document is divided into parts and each member of the team is given one or more parts to write. The parts are assembled in a group editing session, in which members suggest revisions for the entire document. This technique's value is that team members often see things that individual section writers have missed; the resulting suggestions may greatly improve the document.

Team Revision

In the team-revision method, one person writes a document's first draft and then distributes it to other group members, who can then suggest revisions. An important benefit from this process is that the document has one voice or a uniform style rather than seeming to be made of different parts that do not sound alike, which sometimes happens to group-written documents. But having one person write a document can take time, and team members do not have the chance to contribute until the group editing sessions.

A Case History

One year when I was chair of my department's promotion committee, we had five people who were eligible for promotion. We voted to support each candidate for promotion. Then we gave each member of the promotions committee the task of drafting a letter for one (and, in my case, two) candidates.

These drafts were duplicated and given to all committee members. As a group, we then met and critiqued each draft and made many suggestions about how each promotion letter might be improved. These suggestions involved such matters as the words that were used, the structure of the letter, the best way to make the argument for promotion, punctuation, document design, and so on. Although it was a time-consuming and exhausting process, it was very successful: All of our candidates were promoted. And a member of the university's promotions committee told me a year later that our letters were the best the committee had received that year. In this case the process worked, and collaborative writing helped us to be more successful than we would have been individually.

Summary

Brainstorming and collaborative writing are effective and useful techniques. Used intelligently and exploited for what they can contribute to the process of generating ideas, strategies, and resulting documents, they are extremely functional. They enable people to energize one another, they help people bond together, and they are also, it turns out, very efficient and effective tools.

This chapter has dealt with the way brainstorming can be used to develop creative ideas dealing with matters such as revising a department's curriculum or dealing with hostile individuals. We have also considered collaborative writing, a technique that is widely used in the business world as well as in academic settings because it is so functional. We turn next to matters related to the process of writing, such as using time efficiently, organizing documents, and avoiding writer's block.

7 | The Process of Writing

Psychologists tell us that some people work most effectively in the morning and others work best in the afternoons or evenings. Variations on this theme include "larks," who function best early in the morning, and "night owls," who excel late at night. If you are a lark, it makes sense to write in the morning and teach and do research in the afternoon. And if you are an owl or a night owl, it is logical to teach and do your research in the morning or afternoon and write in the evening or late at night (depending on how late you work).

If, by chance, you are involved in a project in which there is collaborative writing, such as a proposal to redesign your department's curriculum, and there are larks and night owls on your team, you will have to work hard to figure out how to accommodate everyone. You may have to divide the work and then come together at some mutually convenient time to put the document together.

Steps in Writing

Writing involves more than finding out when you and your collaborators work best. Time also has other considerations, because writing involves more than sitting down at a typewriter or computer and punching keys. There are three basic steps to the process of writing: (a) planning what is to be written, (b) drafting the document, and (c) editing and rewriting.

This chapter will discuss each topic in detail and also offer suggestions for dealing with writer's block.

Planning What Is to Be Written

When you have to write a document, after you have done your research, gathered your data, and done some thinking about what you want to say, you should prepare an outline that you can follow in writing your document. You will save a great deal of time if you prepare a good outline and follow it, because outlines enable you to see the logical structure of your document; it is much easier to make changes in the organization of your document before rather than after you write.

I outline by brainstorming in my journals and by putting ideas on small slips of paper, one idea per slip. I then assemble the slips into a logical and coherent whole and have my outline. Limiting myself to one idea per piece of paper allows me maximum flexibility. Numerous outlining programs for computers also are available.

Drafting the Document

My personal opinion is that you should never spend more than two or three hours at a time writing. After a few hours, the law of diminishing returns generally sets in: It may take you 30 minutes to write what you would have written in 5 or 10 minutes if you had been fresh.

If you write for two or three hours you will probably end up with five or six pages of written text. The secret of being productive is to be disciplined and to work steadily. When working on a project, write five or six pages a day on the days that you schedule yourself for writing . . . and do not skip a scheduled day.

If you are going to limit the amount of time you spend at each writing session, you must do some planning to give yourself enough days to write your document. If I press myself and write 10 pages in one day, I am usually so tired that I cannot write for days afterward and fall behind my schedule. I generally only write in the mornings, although I can write at any time. The secret of productivity in writing, I believe, is working steadily rather than in long, exhausting writing binges.

I am speaking from personal experience. Some people may be most effective and most productive when they write 12 hours a day, and they may be able to write this way year after year. I would say they are the exceptions. Most people cannot write efficiently for long periods of time, and unless there is some emergency, it is better to do some simple time scheduling and planning than be forced to write for hour after hour because you left everything to the last minute.

In some cases, psychologists tell us, it is best to spend a long time at some project. Learning languages and mathematics apparently are best done in large blocks of time. But if you can plan to write for short periods of time, it is generally best to do so. In addition to the mental fatigue caused by writing, sitting at a typewriter or computer for long periods of time can cause physical discomfort and perhaps even problems.

Editing and Revising the Document

After you have written your first draft, if you have enough time, it is a good idea to put the manuscript aside for a couple of days, so you can look at it with a fresh mind and then start the editing and revising process. The secret of writing is rewriting; every book on writing will tell you that. Very few writers are able to create documents that do not benefit from editing and revising.

It is here that you start polishing your writing; you change words, cut out wordy passages, add transitions, find examples to discuss, and move sentences and paragraphs around to end up with a document that says what you want it to say in the style you want to say it. Editing and revising are best done on hard copy, so print out your drafts, make your revisions on the printouts, and then make them on the copy in your file.

Feedback

It is a good idea when you are doing your planning to allow time to show your document to others to get some feedback. Other readers looking at your document with fresh eyes can often see things you have missed and make suggestions that will improve your document.

How to Avoid Writer's Block

When you write in academic institutions, you always have deadlines to meet. And, of course, writing a report or other document is only one of many things you probably have to do. In some cases, when they do have time to write, people experience so-called writer's block: They cannot seem to get started for one reason or another.

In 30 years of writing, I have hardly ever found myself in a situation where I felt "blocked" and could not write. One reason for this may be my journal keeping. I am used to sitting and writing whenever I have a bit of free time. But people who do not write much do have difficulties getting started on a document. The following suggestions may be helpful to those who have problems starting a writing project.

❶ *Pretend you are writing a letter to a friend about the document.* Write "Dear X" and then start telling your friend about the document. Once you are writing easily, erase the "Dear X."

❷ *Start in the middle of your document; do not wait for the "perfect" opening sentence.* It is this search for the perfect opening sentence that probably causes more blocks in writers than anything else.

Pressure to come up with a document in a limited period of time is another major source of writer's block. You deal with this by planning, which allows you time to write in a more leisurely manner and have time for revisions.

❸ *Try freewriting.* Write without stopping for three minutes on any topic: sports, weather, politics, and so on. That may warm you up and enable you to avoid being blocked.

❹ *Write a letter to a friend to get you going.* This may "rev up your engine," so to speak.

❺ *Brainstorm to get your creative juices flowing.* Then start expanding on what you have been brainstorming about, using the brainstorming as a form of outlining ideas.

Writer's block is caused by many things, including anxiety about finding the perfect opening sentence and concern about doing a great job of writing a document, word by word and line by line. If you adopt a different notion of what writing is like and see it as being like making a drawing—blocking out the general composition and then working over different parts—you might not be bothered by anxiety about perfect openings and getting every word or sentence perfect on the first draft.

Summary

This chapter has considered the actual process of writing. This involves making an outline, writing a first draft, revising the draft on hard copy, and revising and rewriting. It is best not to write for more than two or three hours in a day; this avoids the mental fatigue and physical ailments connected with typing for long periods of time. We can avoid these problems by planning and keeping to a schedule. It also is useful to have others read what you write, offering feedback and suggesting changes that may improve your document.

Now that you have actually written your document, you must give some thought to how it will look in print. Chapter

8 offers a primer on design and layout that will help you produce attractive documents and avoid some of the most common design mistakes.

8 | Layout and Design

The way a document looks plays an important role in the way it is evaluated by readers. Regardless of whom the document is written for, the better it looks the more successful it will be. Good document design or layout is based on keeping in mind (a) the importance of simplicity, (b) the role of "white space," (c) the importance of display, and (d) the role of text design and information graphics. We will now deal with these topics in some detail.

Keep It Simple

The cardinal rule for producing good-looking documents is "keep it simple." This was not much of a problem when most documents were produced by typewriters. All that a typist could do was type lowercase or capital letters, underline, and change the spacing between letters and margins. But these options were quite limited. In the computer age, we now find desktop publishing programs that can do anything one wants in document design and printers that can generate many different typefaces and fonts.

A typeface such as Times Roman could have bold, italic, condensed, and expanded fonts in a variety of sizes (for example, 10 point). This means far more opportunities for producing documents that are visually monstrous, because many people do not have much understanding of the aesthetic aspects of document production.

Generally speaking, a good rule is use no more than two or three typefaces in your documents. Use different typefaces only when display is important and you want to create a particular kind of impression. But remember, if you use too many different faces and fonts, the document looks too busy and becomes visually chaotic. In the field of visual communication, the operating rule is "less is more." The simpler, the better. It is also a good idea to avoid lines, stars, dots, and other such ornaments. Be conservative when it comes to determining the look of your document; the fewer things you do, the less likely you are to make a mistake.

The Importance of White Space

White space refers to "empty" space in a design. When you think about the margins of your document, remember that a document that seems to crowd a page generates negative reactions. We have learned (from advertising and print design) to associate white space with quality, sophistication, and taste. We have quite different reactions to documents that seem to fit on a page without taking up much of it than to documents that leave small margins on the sides, tops, and bottoms—that is, documents that crowd the page. Of course, you do not want to go to the other extreme and have such big left, right, top, and bottom margins that your document seems lost on the page.

You also have to think about the size of typeface you are using for the body of the document and the size of the typefaces you are using for titles and subheads. Headlines that are too large become overbearing and make the text in the body of the document seem somewhat irrelevant.

Both type size and white space affect readability, which is connected to the white space around each letter, rather than

1. Both large and extremely small typefaces are hard to read. Print text in 10- or 12-point type.
2. Long lines of text are hard to read.
3. FULL CAPS ARE HARD TO READ. Use caps and lowercase for text material. Save full caps for headlines and occasional display situations.
4. Italic typefaces are hard to read. Use them judiciously.
5. Typefaces with serifs (the short lines and strokes at the ends of letters) are easier to read than sans serif (literally, "without serif") faces. Use serif faces for text material.
6. Typefaces that are too heavy are overwhelming and irritate readers. Avoid dark, heavy boldface.
7. Avoid reverse printing (white on black) because it is hard to read.
8. Ragged left lines are confusing and hard to read. Use ragged right lines in your text material to avoid gaps between words.
9. Using many typefaces in your text is unattractive and disconcerting. Confine yourself to a few faces.
10. Small margins make your page look too crowded and your lines of text too long to read easily. Be generous with margins on the sides, top, and bottom of the page.
11. Leave enough space between text lines to increase readability, which is based on the amount of white space around letters, not on the size of the typeface.

Figure 8.1. Rules for Printing

the size of the typeface. If you use a large typeface but do not have enough white space around the letters and between the lines, your document will be unattractive and difficult to read. (See Figure 8.1.)

Some word processing programs come with built-in modules that help people who are not artists figure out how to design a good-looking page. When in doubt, err on the side of having large margins on the sides, top, and bottom rather than very narrow ones; use a small typeface, 10 or 12 points, for your text. Also use relatively small type for heads and subheads; large heads and subheads overwhelm text material.

The Importance of Display

In design terms, display has to do with focusing attention on certain elements on a page, such as a title or a chart. In a document, some things are more important than others, and it is useful to help readers see what is important by using display. For example, if there is an important paragraph in a report that suggests a certain course of action should be taken, there are several ways to give this passage display. You can do so by one or more of the following:

- giving it a subhead,
- indenting it farther,
- adding a lot of white space around it,
- printing it in a different type size,
- using a boldface font, or
- putting it in a box.

You must be very discriminating in using display; if used too often, it loses its effectiveness. Display should be reserved for important elements in your documents—those to which you want to call particular importance.

The Role of Text Design and Information Graphics

You can use formatting to call attention to the logic of a passage or the arguments made in it. In a typical paragraph of prose, the basic ideas are often difficult to see and can get visually lost. That is why it is sometimes good to make a chart, showing the basic ideas with which you are dealing. Readers will see the ideas immediately, because they are forced to do so by the page design. In certain occasions, when comparisons and contrasts are made, it is a good idea to show them in a chart of paired oppositions. Such devices must also be used sparingly or they lose their effectiveness. But charts, lists, and tables are very powerful devices; they are also known now as "infographics," because they use graphic techniques to display visual information.

If you want to make certain that your readers pay particular attention to something—your conclusions, important data, interesting comparisons—then it is a good idea to use infographics and text design to force your readers to take notice. Design is a powerful tool that, when used correctly, can make a document attractive, generate favorable impressions, and facilitate reading and comprehension.

Summary

This discussion of document design has focused on the importance of simplicity, white space, and display in the documents we write. The look of a document plays a significant role in the way people assess it, and a handsomely designed and printed document carries with it an air of authority.

Design is our final subject. This little book has dealt with everything from brainstorming to rewriting documents, from the basic elements in memos, letters, reports, and proposals to persuasive writing. The next chapter offers a few parting comments.

9 | Conclusion

We are now at the end of our journey. We have learned something about how to write various kinds of documents, how to write in a readable manner, how to think up ideas and organize them once we have them, how to schedule our time and avoid writer's block, and how to write and revise drafts of our documents. And with our final draft in hand we have learned how to print our documents in a visually appealing manner to enhance their readability and effectiveness.

All of these skills will be of benefit to us as we pursue our careers in academic institutions of every kind, from community colleges to research universities.

Power in the Academy

Many academicians feel that administrators came to coordinate but stayed to command. They also believe that the numbers of administrators—department chairs, deans, directors, vice presidents, and presidents—have grown disproportionately to the growth of teaching faculty, so that universities are now top heavy with administrators and spend too much money and energy running themselves and not enough teaching students and facilitating research.

But if you think of a typical university as the equivalent of a small city, you recognize the need for people to take care of many different things. Most academic institutions have considerable self-governance, and, in principle, it is the faculty members, functioning in various committees and bodies (such as academic senates), who make the basic decisions about the curriculum and personnel issues—subject to the approval of administrators. These decisions, of course, are communicated by memos, letters, reports, and proposals.

All of this academic "business" writing can divert us from teaching and the scholarly work some of us also want to do. But if you develop a facility for writing these documents (which are somewhat formulaic in nature) and you are organized, then you can generally find a way to teach, perform your own scholarly work, and contribute to the operation of your department, school, college, and university.

A Parting Wish

I wish you good fortune and hope that you will find the suggestions in this book helpful. Benjamin Franklin suggested that his rise in the world was the result of his skills with the written word. He rose from obscurity to dine with kings. Your ability to write memos and other kinds of documents may also be the instrument of your success, and you may dine, if not with kings, with provosts—which is almost as good. And if you learn to write these documents really well, you may even become a provost yourself.

APPENDIX 1

Checklist for Writers

Focus. Is your document:
→ focused narrowly enough?
→ directed at your target audience?

Organization. Is your document:
→ logically organized, with one section leading to the next?
→ designed so that the structure "shows"?
→ coherently written, making use of transitions?
→ based on change over time or comparisons and contrasts?

Title. Have you:
→ given your document a title?
→ made your title specific and not generic?
→ used a title that conveys information about your document?

Mechanics. Have you:
→ numbered the pages?
→ underlined the names of books and magazines?
→ put the titles of articles or reports in quotation marks?
→ used information graphics and other visuals when possible?

→ used quote marks when using other people's language?
→ paraphrased material when using other people's ideas?

Grammatical problems. Have you avoided:
→ sentence fragments?
→ run-on sentences?
→ faulty pronoun reference?
→ errors in agreement?
→ spelling errors?
→ incorrect use of commas and punctuation?
→ improper use of adjectives and adverbs?
→ improper division of words (syllabification)?
→ wrong verb tenses?
→ faulty end punctuation?
→ spelling errors?

Writing problems. Have you avoided:
→ awkward writing?
→ unclear writing?
→ repetitious sentence structure?
→ overly complex sentences?
→ incoherent writing?
→ inappropriate or inconsistent tone?
→ wordy writing?
→ inappropriate diction (slang, etc.)?
→ trite phrases?
→ jargon and overly technical language?
→ lack of emphasis?
→ lack of conclusion?

Revisions. Have you:
→ printed out your first draft and made your revision on "hard copy"?
→ left some time between writing and revising?

→ asked others to proofread your document?

→ used a spell checker and a grammar checker on your document?

Design. Have you:

→ paid attention to the visual look of your document?

→ used wide enough margins?

→ double-spaced the copy when appropriate?

→ made use of subheads to break up the copy?

→ not used too large a face for text (making document hard to read)?

→ not made headlines and subheads too large or heavy?

→ kept design simple, avoiding numerous typefaces and ornaments?

→ used "display" to highlight important concepts, passages, and so on?

→ used a laser printer, if possible, or a dark enough face on a dot-matrix printer?

APPENDIX 2

Computer Aids for Writers

The computer has revolutionized many different aspects of life in the United States. Computer chips are now found in all kinds of places, and computer technology is used in our automobiles, television sets, various machines, and many other places. In essence, a computer is a device that can be used to do any number of different things depending on the program that is running the computer and harnessing its power. Word processing programs are among the most important and most widely used kinds of programs for computers, but many others, such as data bases and spreadsheets, also are available. Several programs that aid writers have been developed, and we will briefly examine them also.

This discussion of computers and writing covers different kinds of computers, word processing, aids to writers, and printers.

Computer technology continually changes (new models with new capacities), and the programs that run computers also evolve rapidly, so this discussion deals in generalities. If you know the principles at work, you can understand everything else.

Using Computers to Write

A good deal of writing that is done in organizations (and by individuals) is done using computers, which are replacing electric and electronic typewriters in many offices. Strictly speaking, we do

73

not write with computers but with word processing programs that these computers operate.

Two computer "environments" are dominant: (a) IBM and IBM clones (also known as "personal computers") and (b) Apple Macintoshes, both of which are used for word processing and desktop publishing, among other functions. Other kinds of computers such as Atari, Amiga, and NeXT (and workstations that use UNIX) also are available, but for all practical purposes these two kinds of computers are the ones most often found in businesses and organizations.

The number of word processing programs that can run in the IBM and Macintosh environments is extremely large. Existing programs are continually updated, and new programs are frequently released. (By far the most popular programs are WordPerfect and Microsoft Word.) The main advantage that Macintosh computers had over personal computers was that Macintoshes were simpler to operate, because they used "icons" (images) rather than verbal commands to operate their programs. With the development of Microsoft's Windows software and other programs such as IBM's OS/2, IBM-type personal computers now can run icon-based software programs; the differences between the two environments is much less significant now, at least for word processing.

There are many programs that allow members of organizations to communicate with one another, swap files, collaborate, and so on, and these programs, along with word processing, have had a major impact on the way organizations are run.

The Most Important Aspect of Word Processing

Let me use an analogy to characterize advanced word processing programs such as WordPerfect and Microsoft Word: They are enormous mansions with more than 100 rooms. Each room represents something the program can do: make footnotes, endnotes, outline, merge files, correct spelling, print, and so on. But most people only use 5 or 10 rooms, and the most important room in the house—the room that makes all the difference—is the one in which we actually do the writing of our documents.

In the case of our word processing program, this "room" allows writers to save what they have written on a disk (or some other storage device), call this material back for revision, save the revision, call it back, and on and on. This is extremely important: As almost every writer will attest, the most important thing about writing is rewriting. Very seldom do writers get things right the first time. You always have to revise. Before computers, you would write something, type it out (or have a secretary or someone else type it out), revise it, and then give the revision back to the typist for retyping. This is no longer necessary. With the development of computers and word processing programs, many writers have seen their productivity rise 30% or 40% because they have eliminated the need to wait for one or more retypings.

It is now possible, even with the simplest word processors to (a) type the first draft of a document, (b) save it on a disk or hard drive, (c) print it out, (d) make a revision on hard copy, (e) replace the original file and call back the revised file, (f) print it out, (g) make other revisions, and (h) save the document with the new revisions.

I find that I often make four or five revisions, sometimes more. Thus we can argue that computers make it possible for writers to do better work, because revisions are so easy. Writing at the keyboard is most efficient—that is, type your first drafts directly into the computer—but even if you write your first drafts out in longhand, being able to type a first draft, save it, and then revise it without having to retype the whole document is what is crucial. (For those who have problems typing or writing at the keyboard, there are many excellent and inexpensive computer programs that teach people how to touch-type and write "at the keyboard.")

Notice that I suggested that revisions be made on hard copy—that is, on material that has been printed out. Most writers agree that it is better to make corrections on hard copy than on a computer screen. For some reason, seeing the material in print and being able to cross out words or lines and make corrections in pencil or ink works better than making revisions directly on the computer screen.

Many people do not need a really powerful word processing program. That is why many software manufacturers now offer programs that do not have all the bells and whistles of full-powered programs. These "cut down" versions have all the important features the ordinary writer needs and are considerably less expensive than the full-power models. An example is LetterPerfect, a scaled-down version of WordPerfect 5.1.

But even if you have the use of a full-powered word processor, you probably will find that you only need to learn how to do a half dozen things: starting the program; formatting the page; deciding on spacing; learning to underline, use various typefaces, and use full capitals; saving what you write; and editing your document.

Computers allow us to do many other things, such as create multiple versions of the same document, collaborate with others in writing and other projects (even at a great distance), and communicate with others around the world, for example, through electronic mail and fax transmission.

Other Aids for Writers

If you have ever looked at a computer magazine, you will have discovered that software writers are ingenious in coming up with new programs. But there are only a few program types, or what we might call "program genres," such as word processing, spreadsheets, and data bases. But other programs can organize your life, figure out your income taxes, draw, compose music, and so on.

For writers, a few kinds of software are of particular interest. Notice that I write in rather general terms here; as I mentioned earlier, it is important to understand the principles at work in these programs, and it is both impossible and unnecessary to cover all of the different programs and their various features. Programs that might be of interest, depending on your strengths and weaknesses as a writer, are:

❶ *Spelling and grammar checkers.* These programs check your writing for grammatical mistakes, stylistic infelicities, and so on. They cannot catch all of your mistakes, but they can determine whether you are writing in an overly simple or overly complex style and whether you have made some grammatical errors, and so forth. They "read" your writing, find errors, and offer suggestions to help with clarity, awkwardness, and other problems. Among these programs are Grammatik, RightWriter, and Editor.

❷ *Outliners.* Many word processing programs come with their own outliners, and other programs will also help writers organize their ideas and put them in outline form. Outlining programs vary from relatively simple ones that offer little more than the outlining done by good word processing programs such as Microsoft Word and WordPerfect to programs that help writers think up, organize, and logically assemble their ideas. An example here would be Max-Think. Some programs help people get ideas and often have queries and other features that stimulate thinking as well as aid in conducting research.

❸ *File-description programs.* One problem with many word processing programs—especially older ones—is that only 11 spaces—8 spaces, 1 period, and 3 spaces—are available for file names; this makes it very difficult to remember what is in a given file. This is a serious problem for people who have a large number of files. However, some utility programs for personal computers such as Dirnotes allow writers to use as many as 32 spaces to describe a given file. For example, I save this file in my word processing program as "computer.bus." But with my utility program I can write a much longer description of the file, such as "Appendix: computer aids." Some newer versions of word processing programs also allow writers more space to describe their files.

❹ *Indexing.* This feature enables writers to prepare indexes from their documents. All that a writer need do is indicate which words he or she wants to include in the index and the program will generate an alphabetical index. There is also an excellent program, Indexx, available from the Philosophy Documentation Center at Bowling Green University that enables you to make indexes from hard copy (such as page proofs); the program is very helpful for writers who wish to make their own book indexes.

❺ *Design and layout programs.* Many programs enable computer users to perform rather sophisticated layouts for newsletters, brochures, booklets, and even books. Some of the more important "high end" programs are Aldus Pagemaker, QuarkXpress, and Ventura Publisher. Many drawing programs—such as CorelDraw!, Adobe Illustrator, Harvard Graphics, and Aldus Freehand—also can be used. (If you are serious about desktop publishing, you can subscribe to publications devoted to the subject such as the newspaper *Typeworld* and the magazine *Publish*.) The more powerful word processing programs now incorporate many desktop publishing features, and the line between desktop publishing programs and word processing programs is becoming fainter and fainter.

Printers

Even if you do not have a desktop publishing program, it is important to think about the look of your document. Printers play an important role here. There are two dominant kinds: dot-matrix and laser (and laserlike "page") printers. Dot-matrix printers work by having tiny metal pins form letters, some at very high speeds. Dot-matrix printers generally can print in several typefaces and at different speeds, depending on the face used. In "draft mode," there is relatively low dot density, so these printers often print at more than 200 characters per second. In other modes, with much higher dot density, the printers are much slower: At near letter quality (NLQ), they often print at approximately 40 to 50 characters per second. This is remarkably fast compared to typing but quite slow when compared to laser printers, which often print six to eight pages a minute.

Laser printers and laserlike page printers that generate between four and six pages per minute are now available for less than $1,000. They generally have a print density of 300 dots per square inch and look much better than dot-matrix printed material. Many organizations now have laser printers, which should be used when presentation values are important, because they create documents that look much better than those prepared on dot-matrix printers and also are much faster.

Ink-jet printers, such as the LaserJets manufactured by Hewlett Packard, have a print density of 300 dots per square inch and are almost as good as laser printers. These popular printers sell for as little as $400. They are also much quieter than dot-matrix printers.

It is possible, then, for relatively little money, to get a printer that will produce visually appealing text and graphic material.

APPENDIX 3

Books and Periodicals on Writing

If you are interested in further exploring the subject of writing—not only memos, letters, reports, and proposals but also general prose—then you might wish to consult the following books.

Barthes, R. (1975). *The pleasure of the text* (by R. Miller, Trans.). New York: Hill & Wang.

This book is a philosophical study of writing and reading, written in Barthes's inimitable, subjective, and poetic style. Its collection of short essays of varying lengths is arranged in alphabetical order on such topics as affirmation, emotion, exactitude, obscurantism, subject, and voice and their relation to pleasure. As Barthes writes, "the text you write must prove to me that it desires me. This proof exists: it is writing. Writing is: the science of the various blisses of language, its Kama Sutra (this science has but one treatise: writing itself)."

Brooks, T. (1989). *Words' worth: A handbook on writing and selling nonfiction.* New York: St. Martin's.

Although primarily written for journalists and people who wish to sell written material, the book has many instructive hints about what and what not to do when writing. It has chapters on such topics as leads, transitions, verb usage, using quotations, and voice.

Cook, C. K. (1985). *Line by line: How to improve your own writing.* Boston: Houghton Mifflin.

Written under the auspices of the Modern Language Association, this book "focuses on eliminating the stylistic faults that most often impede reading and obscure meaning." Such errors include needless words, words in the wrong order, equivalent but unbalanced sentence elements, imprecise relations between both subjects and verbs and pronouns and antecedents, and inappropriate punctuation. The book also has two glossaries dealing with the parts of a sentence and with questionable usage.

Nicholson, M. (1957). *A dictionary of American-English usage based on Fowler's Modern English Usage.* New York: Oxford University Press.

Nicholson's book is an important reference that offers definitive advice on correct word usage. Nicholson offers a most amusing quote from Fowler's original book: "It is perhaps, then, rather a duty than a piece of presumption for those who have had experience in word-judging to take any opportunity . . . of helping things on by irresponsible expressions of opinion." Those interested in the subject of language and word usage also will find William Safire's columns worth reading.

Piotrowski, M. V. (1989). *Re:Writing: Strategies and suggestions for improving your business writing.* New York: Harper & Row.

This book deals with memos, letters, reports, and other business documents and covers everything from how to write to how to make documents visually appealing. It also has material on writing for electronic mail (E-mail).

Strunk, W., Jr., & White, E. B. (1972). *The elements of style* (2nd ed.). New York: Macmillan.

This brief book—fewer than 100 pages—contains invaluable advice on the "elementary rules of usage" and the "elementary principles of composition." It also contains material on style and on commonly misused form, words, and expressions. *Elements* is considered a classic and contains advice that all writers should heed.

White, J. (1987). *The grid book: A guide to page planning.* Paramus, NJ: Letraset.

This book contains excellent advice about what (and especially what *not*) to do when printing documents. It contains many illustrations and will help you avoid some of the errors people commonly make in formatting and in typeface usage.

Zinsser, W. (1985). *On writing well: An informal guide to writing nonfiction* (3rd ed.). New York: Harper & Row.

Zinsser's book grew out of a writing course he taught at Yale University and is a widely used text full of excellent practical advice. It deals with topics such as style, language, and the need for unity. It also contains material on professional and business writing and writing with word processors. For Zinsser, "rewriting is the essence of writing.... [P]rofessional writers rewrite their sentences repeatedly and then rewrite what they have rewritten."

Other resources include the newsletter *Communications Concepts*, which offers helpful hints on writing; discusses trends in writing, designing, and publishing; and reviews books on business writing. It is published by Communications Concepts, 2100 National Press Building, Washington, D.C. The company also publishes *Writing Concepts*, a newsletter devoted specifically to writing. Finally, Sage Publications' scholarly journals *Written Communication* and *Journal of Business and Technical Communication* (*JBTC*) may be of interest.

References

Blanchard, B. (1954). *On philosophical style*. Bloomington: Indiana University Press.

Smelser, N. J. (1993). *Effective committee service*. Newbury Park, CA: Sage.

Strunk, W., Jr., & White, E. B. (1972). *The elements of style* (2nd ed.). New York: Macmillan.

White, J. (1987). *The grid book: A guide to page planning*. Paramus, NJ: Letraset.

Zinsser, W. (1985). *On writing well: An informal guide to writing nonfiction* (3rd ed.). New York: Harper & Row.

About the Author

Arthur Asa Berger is Professor of Broadcast Communication Arts at San Francisco State University, where he has taught since 1965. He has published more than 20 books and written more than 100 articles as well as numerous book reviews. He also is an artist; for many years he drew cartoons and comic illustrations for *The Journal of Communication*. This is his second book on writing. His first is *Scripts: Writing for Radio and Television* (1990). His latest book is *An Anatomy of Humor* (1993).